Lucie Stevens

Treasures from the Thames

Ernst Klett Verlag
Stuttgart · Leipzig

Contents

Before you read the story

1 On the shores of the Thames

What kind of things do you think people can find on the shores of the River Thames? Make a mind map.

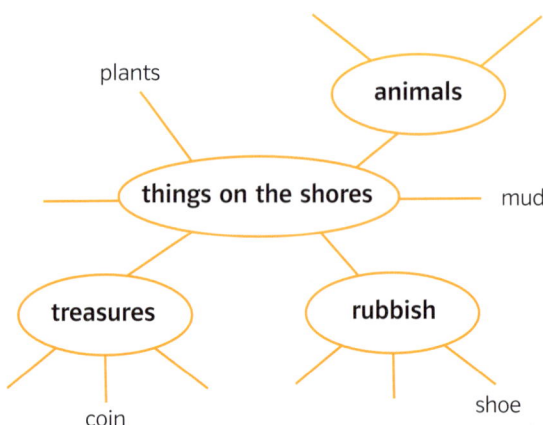

2 The book cover

a) *Look at the cover picture and describe the people in it.*
b) *Where are they?*
c) *What are they doing?*
d) *When does this story take place and how do you know?*
e) *What do you think the story is about?*

3 Finding a treasure

Have you ever found a treasure? What did you do with it? Tell your partner, then listen to his/her story.

1 Almost Easter

It's the Thursday before Easter and a large crowd of people are waiting in Uncle Bertram's pawnshop. It's the largest pawnshop in London, and it's filled with clothes, jewellery and other expensive objects. Today it's also filled with loud voices. The poor are collecting their ₅ clothes from Uncle Bertram's shop because they need them for church the next day. When they don't need their good clothes, the poor often pawn them here, to get money. They talk to each other while they wait until it's their turn. ₁₀

Dorothy has an awful headache, but it's not just from all the noise. She is tired and hungry. She works at the shop for her uncle six days a week. He makes her work very hard, often without a lunch break.

"Hello, Mrs Whitting," Uncle Bertram says to the next ₁₅ woman in the queue. "Your receipt please!"

Mrs Whitting gives him her receipt and he checks his receipt book.

"Eight pennies please," Uncle Bertram says.

"You are a good girl to help your uncle on such a busy ₂₀ day," Mrs Whitting says to Dorothy. She gives Uncle Bertram some coins.

"I don't have a choice," Dorothy says. "Uncle Bertram makes me." Uncle Bertram becomes angry and grabs her wrist. ₂₅

"Hahaa," he laughs. "Dorothy likes to joke. What she means is that she's happy to help her uncle, after everything he does for her. Isn't that right?" Dorothy's wrist hurts, but she doesn't scream.

"Yes, Uncle Bertram," she says. She fakes a smile for ₃₀ Mrs Whitting. "I'm very lucky to have such a nice uncle."

---

2 **pawnshop** [ˈpɔːnʃɒp] Leihhaus • 8 **to pawn sth** [pɔːn] etw. verpfänden •
16 **receipt** [rɪˈsiːt] Quittung • 19 **penny** [ˈpeni] Penny

5

"That's better," Uncle Bertram says. "Now go and get Mrs Whitting's dress."

Dorothy does what Uncle Bertram says because he is often cruel to her and her younger brother Miles without any reason. He's a nasty person who loves money more than anything else, but he doesn't want his customers to know this. So the children must stay quiet about it or they will be in trouble.

The children's father died three months ago. Their mother died nine years ago when Miles was a baby, so they are orphans now. They wanted to live with their grandma in Scotland, but Uncle Bertram wanted them to live with him so they could work in his pawnshop. He liked the idea of free help, so he took the children from their comfortable home in Nottingham and made them move into his house in London. They left so quickly that the children couldn't say goodbye to their friends or neighbours.

Dorothy hurries to a room at the back of the shop with Mrs Whitting's receipt. Miles works in the back room with Uncle Bertram's other assistants to find the right clothes for the right customers. Like Dorothy, Miles is very tired. He is 10 years old and Dorothy is only two years older, but the children don't go to school. Uncle Bertram makes them work for him, but he never gives them any money. He says that some food and a place to sleep is all that they deserve.

Dorothy gives Mrs Whitting's receipt to Miles. She tries not to cry.

"Are you OK?" Miles asks. Dorothy nods. Miles looks over his shoulder to check that nobody is watching, then he gives Dorothy a piece of bread.

---

2 dress [dres] Kleid • **9 to die** [daɪ] sterben • **11 orphan** [ˈɔːfən] Waisenkind • **29 to cry** [kraɪ] weinen • **30 to nod** [nɒd] nicken

"Where did you get this?" Dorothy asks.

"Robert gave it to me," he says. "Eat it quickly before anyone sees."

Dorothy eats the bread while Miles goes to get Mrs Whitting's dress. Robert is the only person at the pawnshop who is nice to the children. Everyone else is too afraid of Uncle Bertram to give the children any food.

Dorothy smiles at Robert to thank him. "Are you looking forward to tomorrow?" he asks. It's Good Friday tomorrow – a holiday.

"Oh yes," Dorothy says. "Miles and I want to go to the park after church."

Suddenly, Robert looks worried and turns away. Uncle Bertram is standing behind Dorothy. He is very angry.

"This is not a picnic!" he shouts. "You are here to work, not talk."

Miles quickly passes Mrs Whitting's dress to Dorothy. He is scared, so Dorothy tries to be brave for her brother. Uncle Bertram follows her as she carries the dress to the front of the shop.

"Sorry to make you wait," he says to Mrs Whitting. "Dorothy is very slow today."

"What a lazy girl you are!" Mrs Whitting says. She points her finger at Dorothy. "You're lucky to have such a nice uncle!"

Dorothy is angry, but she stays quiet. The bell on the door rings and Constable Owens walks in. Everyone in the shop stops talking. Mr Harris, Uncle Bertram's main assistant, takes over so Uncle Bertram can speak to Constable Owens in his office.

When Dorothy gets the clothes for the next customer, she sees that her uncle gives Constable Owens a small leather bag.

---

9 **Good Friday** [gʊd ˈfraɪdeɪ] Karfreitag • 23 **lazy** [ˈleɪzi] faul • 27 **constable** [ˈkʌnstəbl] Polizist/-in, Wachtmeister/-in • 33 **leather** [ˈleðə] Leder

The constable looks very happy. As he passes Dorothy on his way out of the pawnshop, he gives her a nasty look. Dorothy hurries away. Constable Owens is scary, but at least he can't hurt her like Uncle Bertram.

2 The mudlarks

The children get ready for church the next morning in their cold room in the attic. They are hungry and tired because they worked so long the day before, but they're also happy because today is a holiday.

"I have a surprise for you," Miles says. "Close your eyes 5 and hold out your hand."

Dorothy does what Miles says and something drops into her hand. She opens her eyes and – wow! – there are four half-pennies! "Where did you get these, Miles?" Dorothy asks. 10

"From our neighbours," he says. "They pay me a half-penny each week to clean the chicken coop."

"You must hide them," Dorothy says. "Uncle Bertram will take them if he finds out."

"I'll never earn enough money to buy us train tickets 15 to Scotland, so I have made a decision. I want to buy ice creams after church. We can get them from the ice cream man in the park. Uncle Bertram will never know," Miles says.

"But you've worked hard for this money," Dorothy 20 says. "You don't need to spend it on me."

"I want to," Miles says. "We both deserve to have some fun."

Dorothy hugs her brother. She wishes they were back in their warm home, with their father. 25

"You're right," she says. "We do deserve some fun." She gives the coins back to Miles. "Keep them safe in your pocket," she says. "This will be a wonderful day."

• • •

9 **half-penny** [hɒːf ˈpeni] halber Penny • 12 **chicken coop** [ˈtʃɪkɪn ˌkuːp] Hühnerstall • 28 **pocket** [ˈpɒkɪt] (Hosen)tasche

After breakfast, the children wait for Uncle Bertram by the front door. He is wearing his best clothes and is in a great mood. The day before, he made lots of money, which always makes him happy.

5 "Now remember, children," he says as he smiles a nasty smile, "if you're not good at church, I will beat you."

Miles is scared and hides behind Dorothy.

"If you're good, you may go to the park after church," Uncle Bertram says. "But don't forget what will happen if 10 you don't do what I say."

Dorothy nods.

"Good," Uncle Bertram says. He opens the door and walks outside. The children follow. Miles is happier now. As he thinks about eating ice cream, he puts his hand in 15 his pocket and his pennies clink together. Uncle Bertram stops.

"What was that noise?" he asks, quiet and angry. Miles looks at Dorothy and is scared again.

"What noise, Uncle?" Dorothy asks, but she heard the 20 pennies too.

"I know I heard something," Uncle Bertram says. "Turn out your pockets!" Dorothy shows him her handkerchief.

"You see, Uncle? There's nothing," she says. "Maybe you heard a bird."

25 Uncle Bertram glares at her.

"You!" he says, pointing at Miles. Miles looks at Dorothy, but there is nothing she can do to help him. He takes the four half-pennies out of his pocket and shows them to his uncle. Uncle Bertram's face becomes red.

30 "Where did you get this money?" he screams at Miles. He takes the coins and pushes the children back into the house.

"I earned it! I cleaned the neighbours' chicken coop," Miles says. He is so scared that he starts to cry.

---

15 **to clink** [klɪŋk] klimpern • 21 **to turn out** ['tɜːn aut] *hier:* umkrempeln •
22 **handkerchief** ['hæŋkətʃiːf] Taschentuch • 25 **to glare at sb** [gleər] jdn. zornig anstarren

"I don't believe you!" Uncle Bertram shouts. "You don't have time to work for anyone else. You only have time to work for me!"

"No, Uncle," Miles says. "I do it in the morning before breakfast on Mondays and Thursdays." 5

"You're lying!" Uncle Bertram says. "You stole this money from my pawnshop!" Uncle Bertram tries to hit Miles, but Dorothy stands in front of her brother.

"Please, Uncle," she says. "It's Good Friday. Please don't hurt him today." 10

Uncle Bertram lowers his hand, but he is still very angry. "I won't beat you now," he says. "But you will not have a holiday today. You will go to the river and work as mudlarks."

"Yes, Uncle," Dorothy says. She's angry, but she's also 15 happy that Miles is OK.

"Change your clothes and go to the river," Uncle Bertram says, "and if you don't find anything valuable, I will whip you both every night this week."

"Our holiday is ruined," Miles says as he follows 20 Dorothy upstairs to their bedroom.

"It could be worse," Dorothy says. "Maybe today will be our lucky day!"

• • •

It's cold and grey by the river. There are only a few other mudlarks who are looking for money and jewellery 25 in the mud. Most people are at church.

The children work hard all day, but they don't find anything to make Uncle Bertram happy.

"We must go home soon," Dorothy says as she watches the sun go down. "It's getting dark." 30

"But we've only found a few coins," Miles says. "Uncle Bertram will whip us!"

11 **to lower** ['ləʊə] senken • 18 **valuable** ['væljʊəbl] wertvoll

"I know," Dorothy says. "I'm sorry. Maybe he has calmed down now."

"Just a few more minutes," Miles says. "We can still find something."

5 "It's too dark!" Dorothy says. "Let's go."

She takes Miles' hand and pulls him towards the street. A boat goes by which is taking people up the River Thames. Suddenly something shiny near the wall of the embankment catches the boat's lights.

10 "What's that?" Miles asks and points. The children run over to look. Dorothy pulls the shiny thing from the mud. It's a golden locket with red and green jewels on it.

"Wow!" Miles says. "It's so beautiful! It must be worth a lot of money!"

15 "Shh!" Dorothy says. "Don't let the other mudlarks know." She quickly puts the locket in her pocket. "Let's go," she says, and they hurry away.

8 **shiny** [ˈʃaɪni] glänzend • 9 **embankment** [ɪmˈbæŋkmənt] Damm; Uferbefestigung • 12 **golden** [ˈɡəʊldn] golden; aus Gold • 12 **locket** [ˈlɒkɪt] Medaillon • 12 **jewel** [ˈdʒuːəl] Edelstein

3 A new plan

Miles and Dorothy walk home through the dark city streets. They're wet and cold, there's mud all over their clothes and their backs hurt from working all day. But they're too excited to care.

"What will we do with the locket?" Miles asks. 5

"It must be a secret," Dorothy says. "Uncle Bertram will take it if he knows about it."

"But how will we stop him from finding out?" Miles asks.

"We must hide it, but not in the house," Dorothy 10 says. "Mrs Simpkins will find it." Mrs Simpkins is Uncle Bertram's housekeeper and is almost as cruel as he is. She will tell him about the locket if she finds it.

"I know!" Miles says. "Let's hide it in the chicken coop."

"Great idea!" Dorothy says. 15

"But we can't leave it there forever," Miles says.

"Later, we'll sell it to a pawnshop and buy train tickets to Scotland," Dorothy says.

"Maybe even First Class!" Miles says.

"Maybe!" Dorothy says and smiles at her brother. But 20 Miles doesn't smile back.

"Dorothy," he says, "Uncle Bertram pays Constable Owens to keep an eye on the other pawnshops. If we sell it, he'll find out."

Dorothy sighs. "You're right," she says. "Let's hide the 25 locket and work out a plan later."

Miles hides the locket in the neighbours' chicken coop, and the children enter the house through the back door. They look forward to warming up.

---

12 **housekeeper** [ˈhaʊsˌkiːpə] Haushälter/-in • 23 **to keep an eye on sth**
[ˌkiːp_ən_ˈaɪ_ɒn] ein Auge auf etw. haben • 25 **to sigh** [saɪ] seufzen

"Let's make some tea," Dorothy says. Nobody should be in the kitchen now because Mrs Simpkins is having a holiday. But Uncle Bertram is sitting at the table! What is *he* doing in the kitchen?

5 "Hello, Uncle," Dorothy says and pushes Miles behind her. "Did you enjoy church?"

Uncle Bertram ignores her question. "Give me what you found," he says and holds out his hand.

Dorothy gives him the coins they found by the river.

10 "Is this all?" he says.

"Yes, Uncle," Dorothy says. "I'm sorry you're disappointed."

"You and your brother are useless," he says in a nasty voice. "You don't deserve the food I give you. I should 15 throw you out onto the street."

---

7 **to ignore** [ɪgˈnɔː] ignorieren

Dorothy is very angry because Uncle Bertram sold all of her father's things and kept the money. He even sold Father's pocket watch and Mother's wedding ring!

"I have a letter from your grandma," Uncle Bertram says. "She wishes you a Happy Easter." 5

"May we please read the letter?" Dorothy asks and tries to stay calm.

"No," Uncle Bertram says, "but you must write a reply immediately."

Dorothy and Miles look at each other. They know 10 Uncle Bertram hates Grandma's letters.

"Your grandma has invited you to Scotland again, but I will never let you go. Listen to me, you lazy girl! This is what you're going to write in your letter: You're happy in London and you love living with me. She doesn't need to 15 invite you again because you don't wish to go to Scotland. You would never want to leave your nice uncle alone!"

"Yes, Uncle," Dorothy says. She's worried, but she sits down at the kitchen table and Miles sits next to her. Uncle Bertram gives Dorothy some paper and a pencil. 20

"You have one hour to write a reply before I go out for dinner," Uncle Bertram says and leaves the kitchen.

"*You* write the letter," Dorothy says to Miles and opens the kitchen cupboard.

"But Uncle Bertram wants *you* to write it!" he says. 25 "I don't want to make trouble."

"I'll write another letter to Grandma about our plan to run away," Dorothy says as she finds Mrs Simpkins' pencil in the cupboard. "She needs to know that Uncle Bertram is cruel and won't let us go to Scotland. I won't 30 say anything about the locket. We'll tell her about it when we get there."

"But Uncle Bertram will see your letter!" Miles says.

---

3 **pocket watch** ['pɒkɪt ˌwɒtʃ] Taschenuhr • 3 **wedding ring** ['wedɪŋ ˌrɪŋ] Ehering

"We'll hide it between the pages of your letter," Dorothy says.

"It's too dangerous," Miles says.

Dorothy looks at him. "We must try. If Grandma knows
5 the truth she can help us."

When both letters are ready, Dorothy hides hers between the pages of Miles' letter.

"Wait here," she says to Miles. Then she takes the letter to her uncle. Her heart is beating fast.

10 "We've finished, Uncle," she says. "Do you have an envelope?"

Uncle Bertram puts down his newspaper and grabs the letter from Dorothy. "I told *you* to write this letter, girl! Why did *Miles* write it?" he asks.

15 Dorothy thinks quickly. "He needs to practise his spelling, Uncle, so he can write notes for the customers," she says.

Uncle Bertram reads the first page of Miles' letter. Dorothy hopes he won't read the whole letter, but he is
20 suspicious. Then his face turns red.

"What is this?" he says, holding up her letter. "A plan to run away? You have no money!"

"Miles and I want to live with Grandma," Dorothy says and her heart beats even faster.

25 "You are stupid children!" Uncle Bertram shouts. "You and your brother will go to bed without eating dinner. I'll lock you in your room until morning so you can't get food from the kitchen."

Uncle Bertram calls Miles. Then he marches the
30 children to their room and locks them in.

"What are we going to do?" Miles asks.

"I don't know," Dorothy says, "but at least the locket is safe."

---

5 truth [truːθ] Wahrheit • **11 envelope** [ˈenvələʊp] Briefumschlag • **12 newspaper** [ˈnjuːzˌpeɪpə] Zeitung • **20 suspicious** [səˈspɪʃəs] *hier:* misstrauisch • **27 to lock sb in sth** [lɒk] jdn. in etw. einschließen • **29 to march sb to a room** [mɑːtʃ] jdn. in ein Zimmer führen

4 Nigel's newspaper

The next morning, Mrs Simpkins opens the bedroom door. It's the Saturday before Easter. The children must work at the pawnshop, but it won't be very busy. Most people are on holiday today.

The children go downstairs to the kitchen, where Mrs 5 Simpkins has left some bread on the table for them. Miles is very hungry and eats his bread quickly. Dorothy is hungry too, but she only eats half of her bread.

There's a knock on the back door. Mrs Simpkins opens the door and Nigel, the children's friend, is standing 10 there. He's a small boy and his face is always dirty. He works for a newspaper vendor. It's a hard job and Nigel's work day is very long. He collects the newspapers early in the morning, when it's still dark. Then he takes them to the train station in time for the first train of the day. 15 Next, he delivers newspapers to people in the city before they eat breakfast. In the middle of the day he sleeps. But then he must collect the evening newspaper and deliver it all over the city. So much hard work makes Nigel tired. But he is an orphan too, so he *must* work. 20

"Good morning, Mrs Simpkins," Nigel says to the housekeeper. "Here's your newspaper." He gives her the newspaper and she pays him. As Mrs Simpkins closes the door, Dorothy gives Nigel a small nod. Mrs Simpkins takes the newspaper to Uncle Bertram. As soon as she's 25 gone, Dorothy opens the door again.

"Hello Nigel," she says. "I kept this for you." Dorothy gives Nigel half of her bread.

"Thank you so much," he says and takes the bread. "You're a good friend." 30

---

9 **knock** [nɒk] Klopfen • 12 **newspaper vendor** [ˈnjuːzˌpeɪpər ˌvendɔ:] Zeitungs-händler • 16 **to deliver newspapers** [dɪˈlɪvə] Zeitungen austragen • 24 **to give sb a nod** [ɡɪv ˈsʌmbədiˌa ˌnɒd] jdm. zunicken

Dorothy smiles. "We all need to look after each other," she says.

"You're right," Nigel says. He smiles back as he waves and leaves. Lots of people are waiting for their newspapers, so he must hurry.

Mrs Simpkins returns to the kitchen. "Your uncle wants to see you," she says.

The children look at each other, scared.

"Now!" Mrs Simpkins says.

The children hurry to Uncle Bertram's dining room. The smell of eggs and bacon makes Dorothy's stomach rumble.

"Good morning, Uncle," she says. "How are you today?"

Uncle Bertram smiles. "I'm very well, thank you Dorothy," he says. The children are surprised.

"It's a wonderful day," he says, "so wonderful that you won't work at the pawnshop today."

---

4 **to wave** [weɪv] winken • 10 **dining room** [ˈdaɪnɪŋ ˌruːm] Esszimmer • 11 **smell** [smel] Geruch • 12 **to rumble** [ˈrʌmbl] *hier:* knurren

"Oh wow!" Miles says. "Thank you, Uncle!" But Dorothy is suspicious. Their uncle is never nice.

"You're welcome, Miles," Uncle Bertram says. "Aren't I good to you?"

"Yes, Uncle!" Miles says. 5

"Dorothy?" Uncle Bertram says. He gives her a nasty smile.

"You are good to us, Uncle," Dorothy says. She hates him very much.

"I'll let you spend all day outside," he says. "Won't that 10 be fun?"

"Oh yes," Miles says. "It will be wonderful!"

"It *will* be!" Uncle Bertram says. "You will spend the day by the river, working as mudlarks!" Uncle Bertram laughs. He enjoys being cruel to the children. Miles is 15 upset. He doesn't like to be tricked.

"Is the pawnshop closed today?" Dorothy asks.

"No," Uncle Bertram says. "The newspaper has reported that a young woman lost her locket yesterday, by the river near Big Ben. I want you to find it for me." 20

Dorothy and Miles look at each other. It must be the locket they found!

"Do you know the woman?" Dorothy asks.

"No," Uncle Bertram says. "I'll sell the locket on the black market and make lots of money. Now hurry up! 25 The woman is offering a reward, so lots of people will be looking for the locket."

"A reward?" Dorothy asks. She and Miles look at each other again. With the reward money, they could buy train tickets to Scotland! 30

"Yes," Uncle Bertram says. "But don't get any ideas. The police won't give the reward to you. You are children. They would only give it to me. Now hurry along. I want that locket!"

---

16 **to trick sb** [trɪk] jdn. täuschen • 19 **to report** [rɪˈpɔːt] berichten • 25 **black market** [blæk ˈmɑːkɪt] Schwarzmarkt • 26 **reward** [rɪˈwɔːd] Belohnung

5 The lost locket

After the children have changed their clothes, they walk through the streets of London to the River Thames. Miles is upset.

"I wish we could tell the police we have the locket," he says, "but then Constable Owens will find out and ruin everything. It's so unfair!"

"Hmm …" Dorothy says. "Maybe, if we can find out who the young woman is, we can take the locket to her. Then we'll get the reward!"

"Yes! Great idea! Maybe one of our friends knows where she lives," Miles says.

"Maybe," Dorothy says. "But we mustn't ask too many questions. Our friends will become suspicious."

"You'll know what to do, sister," Miles says. "You're clever." Dorothy smiles at her brother.

"We'll find a way," she says. "Grandma will be proud of us."

• • •

There's a crowd of people at the River Thames. Every mudlark in London is looking for the locket.

"Dorothy," Miles says, "do we *have to* work as mudlarks today? We won't find the locket here. Why don't we go to the park?"

"That's a great idea, Miles," she says and smiles. "We can have a holiday after all!"

The children are about to leave when they notice someone in a long coat who is watching the mudlarks on the riverbank. *Constable Owens!*

"Oh no!" Dorothy says. "That awful man! We'll *have to* work now, or he'll tell Uncle Bertram we weren't here."

6 **unfair** [ˈʌnˈfeə] unfair • 25 **to be about to do sth** [biː ə,baʊt tə ˈduː ˌsʌmθɪŋ] kurz davor sein, etw. zu tun • 26 **coat** [kəʊt] Mantel • 27 **riverbank** [ˈrɪvə bæŋk] Ufer

The children are disappointed, but then they see their friends Bea, Nellie and Charles.

"Were you at church yesterday?" Nellie asks. "We didn't see you."

"We had to work," Dorothy replies. 5

"Was the pawnshop open?" Charles asks.

"No. We worked as …" Miles says, but Dorothy stops him.

"We still had to work," she says as she glares at Miles to keep him quiet. "You know what our uncle is like." 10

The other children nod. Their parents are dead too, but they live with their grandad. He is a nice man and never beats them. They only go without food when there is nothing to eat.

"So you haven't found the locket yet?" Dorothy asks. 15

"No, not yet," Nellie replies. "I hope we find it. We could buy so much food with the reward!"

"And new shoes!" Charles says. He holds up his foot. There is a big hole in his shoe, but the children laugh. They all have holes in their shoes. 20

"Did you read about the locket in the newspaper?" Dorothy asks.

"Grandad read it to us," Charles says. "There was even a drawing of the locket with the report."

"What does it look like?" Dorothy asks. 25

"Oh, it's beautiful!" Bea says. "It's golden and has red and green jewels on the front."

Miles looks up at Dorothy. His eyes shine with hope.

"Did the report include the young woman's name?" Dorothy asks. 30

"No," Charles says.

"Did it say where she lives?" Dorothy asks. Charles shakes his head.

---

11 **parents** *(pl)* ['peərəntz] Eltern *(pl)* • 33 **to shake** [ʃeɪk] schütteln

"Why do you have so many questions?" says someone who is standing behind Dorothy. She turns around. 'Oh no!' she thinks. It's Tom and Frank, the nasty boys who work for the butcher.

5 "Clever people always have lots of questions," Dorothy says.

"Are you saying we're not clever?" Frank asks.

"Did you hear me say that?" Dorothy says. Tom and Frank are very angry and Tom raises his fist to hit Dorothy.

10 "What's going on here?" a man asks. It's Constable Owens.

"Nothing, Constable," Tom says. Then he and Frank run away.

"Shouldn't you be working?" Constable Owens asks
15 Dorothy. "Your uncle will be disappointed if you don't find anything."

"Yes, Constable," Dorothy says. She digs into the mud. Constable Owens watches her for a long time, before he walks away.

20 "Do you think he heard your questions?" Miles whispers when the constable has gone.

"I hope not," Dorothy says, "or he'll tell Uncle Bertram."

• • •

By the afternoon, many of the mudlarks are disappointed that they haven't found the locket. Miles
25 has found a key and Dorothy has found a hatpin. But Uncle Bertram won't be happy when they arrive home without the locket. It won't be safe in the chicken coop for long. The children must find out who the young woman is before it's too late. But who will know her
30 name, besides the police?

---

4 **butcher** ['bʊtʃə] Schlachter • 9 **fist** [fɪst] Faust • 17 **to dig** [dɪg] graben •
25 **hatpin** ['hætpɪn] Hutnadel • 30 **besides** [bɪ'saɪdz] *hier:* außer

"That's it!" Dorothy shouts. Everyone on the riverbank looks at her.

"Did you find the locket?" Nellie asks. She looks very excited.

"No!" Dorothy says quickly. "I mean, that's it! I've had enough! Come on Miles, we're going home." 5

"But …" Miles says. Dorothy takes his hand and walks away.

"What's going on?" he asks, when they're back on the street. 10

"I have an idea," Dorothy says. "Let's talk to Nigel! The report about the lost locket was in the newspaper. That means someone who works for the newspaper spoke to the young woman. Maybe Nigel can find out who she is."

"Great idea!" Miles says. "He'll be at the publisher's 15 office now, waiting for the evening newspaper."

The children hurry through the streets. They are excited. Nigel is their good friend, so they can trust him.

The publisher's office is full of boys like Nigel. They joke and laugh with each other while they wait. It's 20 very loud, with so many boys and the machines that are printing newspapers. Miles and Dorothy find Nigel sleeping under a table and Dorothy shakes him.

"Am I late?" he asks.

"No. Don't worry!" Dorothy says. "Sorry to wake you 25 up."

"How can you sleep in this noise?" Miles asks.

"I'm used to it," Nigel says. "What are you doing here? Is everything OK?"

"We need your help," Dorothy says. She explains that 30 they found the locket from the newspaper and want to find the owner without going to the police. Nigel is amazed that they have the locket. Dorothy and Miles are always good to him, so he wants to help them.

18 **to trust** [trʌst] vertrauen • 22 **to print** [prɪnt] drucken • 25 **to wake sb up** [ˈweɪk ˌsʌmbədi ˌʌp] jdn. aufwecken • 32 **to be amazed** [biː əˈmeɪzd] verblüfft sein

"Meet me after church tomorrow," he says. "I'll try to find out who the young woman is."

"Thank you," Dorothy says. "We'll bring the locket to church, so we can take it to the woman if you find out 5 where she lives. Make sure nobody knows what you're doing."

"I won't tell anyone," Nigel says. "You can trust me."

Dorothy and Miles walk home from the publisher's office. They're excited. Maybe they'll get the reward after 10 all! But as they reach their street, something catches Miles' eye. "Oh no!" he says.

"What?" Dorothy asks.

"I think I saw a man in a long coat and I think he was following us," he says. The children look behind them, 15 but there are too many people on the street to be sure.

"I hate Constable Owens," Dorothy says as they reach Uncle Bertram's house.

6 An important clue

The next day, the children stand beside Uncle Bertram at church. They're on their best behaviour, so they keep their eyes on their song books. Miles is nervous, but Dorothy is in a good mood. She finds it difficult to stay quiet because she is so excited. 5

Nigel is at the back of the church with the other orphans. Dorothy is careful not to wave or smile at him. If Constable Owens followed the children home from the publisher's office yesterday, Uncle Bertram will already be suspicious. 10

Before they left for church, Uncle Bertram told the children that they must work in the pawnshop later that day. Many people want to pawn their clothes in the afternoon because Easter services finish in the morning. But Uncle Bertram isn't going to work today. He's going 15 to eat lunch with his friends. This is good news for the children, because Uncle Bertram won't know that they aren't at work.

When church has finished, Uncle Bertram takes the children outside. 20

"Mr Harris will be waiting for you at the pawnshop at exactly 12:30 p.m.," he says. "Go home, change into your work clothes, eat lunch, then be there on time."

"Yes, Uncle Bertram," the children say. It's difficult for Miles to lie, but there is no other way. 25

"Tonight Mr Harris will tell me how much money the shop made and how you behaved," Uncle Bertram says. "Make sure you work hard."

Miles looks at Dorothy. He's very worried now. Uncle Bertram will find out if they don't go to work. 30

"Now go on! Hurry up!" Uncle Bertram says as he walks away.

---

2 **to be on one's best behavior** [biː ˌɒn wʌnz best bɪˈheɪvjə] sich gut benehmen •
14 **service** [ˈsɜːvɪs] *hier:* Gottesdienst • 27 **to behave** [bɪˈheɪv] sich benehmen

"Oh, Uncle!" Dorothy calls after him. Miles holds his breath. What is his sister doing?

Uncle Bertram turns around. He looks angry. "What?" he shouts.

5 "Happy Easter!" Dorothy says as she smiles her sweetest smile. Uncle Bertram shakes his fist at her, so Dorothy grabs Miles' hand and hurries towards the graveyard behind the church.

"Are you crazy?" Miles says. "He'll know that something 10 is going on now!"

"I don't care!" Dorothy says. "I'm too excited. Today could be our lucky day!"

"I wish we could visit Father's grave today," Miles says as the children walk through the graveyard and look for 15 Nigel.

"Me too," Dorothy says. "But Uncle Bertram will never let us travel back to Nottingham."

"I know," Miles says. "I miss our old house in Nottingham, and my old friends. I even miss school!"

20 Dorothy puts her arm around her brother. "When we're in Scotland, you can go to school again. School is very important," she says. "And I'll find a job so we can give Grandma some money."

The children hear a whistle that is coming from behind 25 a tree. They know it's Nigel, and they hurry over to him.

"Happy Easter, Nigel!" Miles says.

"Did you find out who she is?" Dorothy asks. She's too excited to be polite.

"Yes, I did!" Nigel says. "I found the publisher's receipt 30 book. It records the name and address of everyone who has placed a notice in the newspaper."

"Wonderful!" Miles says. Their plan could really work!

"And?" Dorothy asks.

---

1 **to hold one's breath** [həʊld wʌnz 'breθ] die Luft anhalten • 8 **graveyard** ['greɪvˌjɑːd] Friedhof • 11 **I don't care!** [ˌiː dəʊnt 'keər] Mir doch egal! • 13 **grave** ['greɪv] Grab • 24 **whistle** ['wɪsl] Pfeiffen • 31 **notice** ['nəʊtɪs] *hier:* Anzeige

"Her name is Miss Adeline Illingsworth of Belgrave Square. She placed a notice in yesterday's newspaper," Nigel says.

"Well done, Nigel!" Dorothy says.

"Are you sure it's her?" Miles asks. "If we take the locket to the wrong address, the police will find out we have it."

"I *am* sure," Nigel says. "It was the only notice yesterday."

"Thank you so much, Nigel!" Dorothy says. "If we have any reward money left after we've bought our train tickets, we'll give it to you."

Nigel's face turns pink. He's very happy. But he's also sad that his friends will move to Scotland.

"There's just one problem," Dorothy says. "I don't know the way to Belgrave Square."

"I don't know either," Nigel says.

"What will we do?" Miles asks. A bell tolls. It's already eleven o'clock. The children don't have much time before Mr Harris will notice that they are missing.

5 "I know!" Nigel says. "My friend Edwin delivers newspapers to the rich. We'll ask him where Belgrave Square is."

"Great!" Dorothy says. "Where is he now?"

Nigel looks at the blue sky. The sun is warm, even 10 though spring has only just started.

"Probably in the park, near the publisher's office," he says.

"Great!" Dorothy says. "Let's take the backstreets. Constable Owens is probably looking for us."

15 The children hurry out of the graveyard and Nigel leads them through the backstreets of London. He knows the area from delivering his newspapers. Dorothy and Miles have never been in these streets. There's lots of rubbish outside the doors.

20 "I don't like it here," Miles says as he follows Nigel.

The children go around a corner. This street smells awful! There are lots of rats eating rubbish and lots of cats chasing rats.

"Are we near the butcher's shop?" Dorothy asks.

25 "Yes," Nigel says. "It's the fastest route."

"Oh no!" Miles says. "What if Tom and Frank see us?"

"It'll be OK," Dorothy says. "Let's run fast!"

The children run as quickly and quietly as they can past the back door of the butcher's shop. But the street is 30 wet and Miles falls down.

"Ouch!" he cries. Dorothy helps him up quickly, but it's too late. The butcher's boys hear them.

"Hey, Frank!" Tom says. "There are some dirty orphans in the street!"

1 **not … either** [nɒt … 'aɪðə] auch nicht • 2 **to toll** [təʊl] läuten • 9 sky [skaɪ] Himmel • 13 **backstreet** ['bækstriːt] kleine Seitenstraße • 15 **to lead** [liːd] führen • 21 **to smell** [smel] riechen

"Let's get them!" Frank says. The children run, but Frank and Tom chase them.

"Oh no!" Miles shouts. His legs hurt. Dorothy takes his hand and makes him run faster. The butcher's boys are getting closer. 5

"Down here!" Nigel shouts and runs around a corner. But a huge dog jumps onto the street. It barks at the children and blocks their way. Frank and Tom are behind them now. There's nowhere else to go.

"We've got you now," Tom says with a nasty smile. 10

"What do you want?" Dorothy asks.

"We think you have something that is worth a lot of money," Frank says.

"I don't know what you're talking about," Dorothy says.

"Then you won't miss it if we take it," Tom says. He and 15 Frank grab Dorothy and pull off her hat and shawl. Nigel and Miles try to stop them, but they are much smaller than the other boys.

"Get away from her!" Miles shouts, but the butcher's boys ignore him. They pull at Dorothy's clothes to see 20 if she is wearing the locket. Dorothy screams and kicks, but the boys won't let her go.

"What's going on here?" a young man shouts. He grabs Tom's arm and pulls him away from Dorothy. Then he pushes Frank onto the ground. It's Henry, the blacksmith. 25

"Get out of here before I call the police," he says as he points his big hammer at the butcher's boys.

Tom and Frank look at Henry's hammer and run away.

"Henry – you saved us!" Nigel says. "Thank you so much!" 30

Nigel and Henry are friends. Like Dorothy, Henry often gives Nigel food.

"Are you OK, Miss?" Henry asks Dorothy. He helps her stand up.

---

16 **shawl** [ʃɔːl] Schultertuch · 25 **blacksmith** [ˈblæksmɪθ] Schmied · 26 **Get out of here!** [ˌget ˈaʊt əv ˌhɪər] Verschwindet!

"Yes, I am. Thank you," she says. "Miles, are you OK?"

Miles nods. "I haven't lost it," he says and pulls a piece of string from under his shirt. The locket hangs from it. The children thought it was safer for Miles to carry the
5 locket and they were right.

"Wow!" Henry says. "That looks expensive!"

"They found it," Nigel says. "We're taking it back to a young woman to get the reward."

But something about the locket is different now.

10 "It's broken," Miles says. Dorothy looks more closely.

"No, it isn't," she says. "It can open."

Inside the locket is a lock of dark hair. "Look at the hair!" Dorothy says. "The locket must mean a lot to the woman."

15 "Yes," Miles says, "like Mother's ring and Father's watch …"

"And everything else that Uncle Bertram sold," Dorothy says. The children look at each other sadly.

"Now it's even more important that we bring it back
20 to the young woman," Miles says. "I don't want Uncle Bertram to sell it on the black market. He doesn't care about other people at all."

In the distance, a bell tolls. It's 11:45 a.m. already!

"We don't have much time left," Dorothy says. "We
25 must take the locket to Belgrave Square before Mr Harris notices we're missing."

"But we still don't know where Belgrave Square is," Miles says.

"Willie can help you," Henry says. "I've just fixed the
30 wheel on his cart."

"Does he know the way?" Nigel asks.

"I'm sure he does," Henry says. "He delivers milk all over the city."

2 **piece of string** [piːs ɒv ˈstrɪŋ] Stück Schnur • 3 **shirt** [ʃɜːt] Hemd • 3 **to hang** [hæŋ] hängen • 12 **lock** [lɒk] *hier:* Locke • 30 **cart** [kɑːt] Wagen; Karren

Henry leads the way to his workshop, where Willie is harnessing his horse to his cart.

"Willie, can you take these children to Belgrave Square?" Henry asks. "They must get there as quickly as possible." 5

"Of course I can," Willie says. "I'm going home that way. Jump on!"

Dorothy looks at the cart. "Can we sit in the back? Nobody will see us there," she says.

Willie is worried. "Are you in trouble?" he asks. 10

"Don't worry," Nigel says. "They're good people."

"They don't look like they belong in Belgrave Square," Willie says. He's right. Dorothy's dress is torn and Miles is covered in mud from the street.

"Oh no," Miles says. "Nobody will let us speak to Miss 15 Adeline like this!"

"Don't worry about that now," Dorothy says. "Let's just get to Belgrave Square."

1 **workshop** ['wɜːkʃɒp] Werkstatt • 2 **to harness a horse (to a cart)** ['hɑːnɪs] ein Pferd (an einen Wagen) anspannen • 13 **torn** [tɔːn] zerrissen

7 Belgrave Square

Dorothy and Miles keep their heads low as they sit in the back of the cart. They don't want anyone to see them, especially now that Tom and Frank think they have the locket.

5 "Those boys are cleverer than I thought," Dorothy says to Miles. "I asked too many questions on the river bank."

"You had to!" Miles says. "And anyway, those boys are always looking for trouble."

After a while, the cart stops. "We're here," Willie
10 whispers over his shoulder. He has stopped across the street from Miss Adeline's home.

Dorothy helps Miles climb out of the cart. But just as they are about to cross the street, a man in a dark coat walks into the square. *Constable Owens!* Dorothy pulls
15 Miles behind the cart so that the police officer can't see them.

"Has he gone?" she whispers to Willie.

"Yes!" Willie says when he can't see the police officer any more.

20 "He must know something," Dorothy says. "Why else would he be here?"

"What will he do to us if he sees us?" Miles asks.

"I don't know," Dorothy says. "Let's hope we don't find out."

25 The children cross the wide street of Belgrave Square as quickly as possible. It's a beautiful area with white buildings and a large park.

"Miss Adeline must have lots of money," Miles says. "Do you think she'll listen to us?"

30 "Of course!" Dorothy says, but she isn't really sure. The children hold each other's hands as they enter Miss Adeline's front garden. They're both nervous.

"We can do this," Dorothy says. "Soon we'll be with Grandma." Miles smiles and nods.

The children walk to the front door of Miss Adeline's beautiful house and ring the doorbell. Miles holds his breath as the door opens. 5

A tall man in a black suit looks down at them. "Who are you?" he asks.

"Please, Sir," Dorothy says. "We need to speak to Miss Adeline."

The man looks angry. "Beggars aren't welcome here," 10 he says. "Go away!"

"Please, Sir," Dorothy says again. But the man just closes the door.

4 **doorbell** [ˈdɔːrbel] Türklingel • 6 **suit** [suːt] Anzug • 8 **Sir** [sɜː] Herr • 10 **beggar** [ˈbegə] Bettler/-in

"What are we going to do, Dorothy?" Miles asks.

"Let's try the kitchen door," Dorothy says. "Maybe the housekeeper will listen to us."

The children walk down the side of the house to the ⁵ servants' door and knock. A young man opens the door.

"Hello," Dorothy says. "We need to speak to Miss Adeline. It's very important! We have information about her missing locket."

The young man looks surprised. "Come in," he says.

¹⁰ While he finds the housekeeper, the children wait in the kitchen. There are many servants and they're preparing a large meal. It smells wonderful. Miles' stomach rumbles as the bell tolls 12:15 p.m. Only fifteen minutes until Mr Harris will notice that they aren't at the pawnshop!

¹⁵ A door opens, but it isn't the young man with the housekeeper. It's the angry, tall man who was at the front door.

"What are you doing in here?" he shouts at the children. "I told you to go away!"

²⁰ "We're waiting for the housekeeper," Dorothy says. "We need to speak to Miss Adeline about her locket."

"I told you already," the man says. "Beggars aren't welcome here."

He marches across the kitchen and grabs the children ²⁵ by the ears. Then he drags them out of the door and pulls them onto the street.

"Ah ha! Just what we need! Constable!" he calls to a police officer who's walking near the park. *It's Constable Owens!*

³⁰ "Oh no!" Miles says.

"Please listen to us," Dorothy says. But the man in the suit ignores her. Constable Owens sees the children and crosses the street.

---

5 **servant** ['sɜːvənt] Diener/-in • 25 **ear** [ɪər] Ohr • 25 **to drag** [dræg] schleppen

"What have these children done?" he asks the man.

"I am the butler for Miss Adeline Illingsworth," the man replies. "These children were trespassing."

"I see," Constable Owens says. "How lucky I was here. I'll take them to the police station." 5

"Thank you, Constable," the butler says, "and Happy Easter!"

"Hello children," Constable Owens says as soon as the butler has gone. He doesn't sound at all friendly. "How interesting to find you here in Belgrave Square." 10

"We were taking a walk before work," Dorothy says.

"Don't lie to me!" Constable Owens says. He handcuffs the children together. Then he pulls off Dorothy's shawl. 'He's looking for the locket!' Dorothy thinks. But just like Tom and Frank, Constable Owens doesn't think that 15 Miles will have the locket. For the moment at least, it is safe. But it won't be safe for much longer.

---

2 **butler** ['bʌtlə] Butler · 3 **to trespass** ['trespəs] unbefugt betreten ·
12 **to handcuff sb** ['hændkʌf] jdm. Handschellen anlegen

8 The woman in the violet dress

"Let's go," Constable Owens says. "As soon as you're locked up at the police station, I'll find your uncle."

Miles looks at Dorothy. He hopes she has a plan to save them. But what can she do? If they run away, Constable
5 Owens will catch them. And even if he doesn't, where will they go? If they return to Miss Adeline's, the butler will call the police.

As they come to a corner, Constable Owens pushes the children. They bump into a young woman in a beautiful,
10 shiny violet dress.

The woman's purse falls from her hand and everything inside it falls onto the street. "Oh dear!" the woman cries.

"Sorry, Miss," Miles says.

"It was an accident, Miss," Dorothy says. "The
15 constable pushed us."

The woman looks at the children and then at Constable Owens.

"Sorry, Miss," Constable Owens says. "These children are wild. I'm taking them to the police station."

20 The woman isn't impressed. "If you can't even control two children, how will you keep us safe?" she says.

Even though she's in so much trouble, Dorothy laughs. The woman is very clever. Constable Owens is embarrassed. He doesn't know what to say.

25 "Can I help you, Miss?" Miles asks. He starts to pick up the woman's things with the hand that isn't handcuffed.

"Watch them!" Constable Owens says as he pushes the children away. "They're thieves!"

"We are not thieves!" Dorothy says. "We were just
30 trying to speak to Miss Adeline Illingsworth. It's very important!"

---

violet ['vaɪələt] violett; lila • **9 to bump into sb** [bʌmp] mit jdm. zusammen-
stoßen • **11 purse** [pɜːs] Portemonnaie • **20 to control** [kənˈtrəʊl] *hier:* bändigen •
28 thief [θiːf] Dieb/-in

"I am Adeline Illingsworth," the woman says. "Why do you need to speak to me?"

"Don't bother this woman," Constable Owens says to Dorothy. He tries to march the children away, but Miss Adeline stops him.

"Constable," she says. "I would like the children to answer my question."

"But I'm taking them to the station," the police officer says.

"Why?" Miss Adeline asks.

"They were trespassing," Constable Owens says in an angry voice, "at *your* house. You should thank me for keeping your home safe."

Miles suddenly feels brave. Miss Adeline is here and she wants to listen to them. Now is their only chance!

"We weren't trespassing, Miss," he says. "We wanted to give this to you."

Miles pulls the locket out from under his shirt. Constable Owens will tell Uncle Bertram that the children had the locket all along, but Miles doesn't care. It's more important that Miss Adeline gets her locket back.

"My locket!" Miss Adeline cries.

"You awful children!" Constable Owens says. "Wait until I tell your uncle!"

"Tell him," Dorothy says and smiles at Miles. She's proud of him. "We're happy we've saved Miss Adeline's locket from the black market."

"What do you mean?" Miss Adeline asks.

"Don't listen to them, Miss," Constable Owens says. "These children only tell lies."

But Miss Adeline doesn't believe him. She looks down at the children. Miles is still holding the locket.

"Please take it," he says to her. "It's yours."

---

3 **to bother sb** [ˈbɒðə] jdn. belästigen • 20 **all along** [ˌal əˈlɒŋ] die ganze Zeit

"Our uncle wants to sell it and make lots of money," Dorothy says.

"We didn't want you to lose it forever," Miles says. Miss Adeline's eyes fill with tears.

5 "Oh, you wonderful children," she says. She takes the locket and holds it to her heart. "How can I ever thank you?"

"Please don't let Constable Owens take us to the police station," Miles says. "Our uncle will beat us when he
10 knows we have given the locket back to you."

"Don't believe them, Miss," Constable Owens says. "Their uncle is a good man."

But Miss Adeline has already decided who to believe. "Let these children go immediately," she says, "or I will
15 report you to the Head of Police. I know him. I talked to him about my locket." Constable Owens is too scared to reply. "Constable," Miss Adeline says, "didn't you hear me?"

Constable Owens is angrier than the children have
20 ever seen him. But he takes the handcuffs off them.

"Off you go then," Miss Adeline says to the police officer. Constable Owens opens his mouth, but doesn't know what to say. He turns around and hurries down the street.

25 "We did it!" Dorothy cries. She hugs her brother. "I'm so proud of you! You're so brave!"

Miles starts to cry, but this time it's because he's so happy.

"What good children you are," Miss Adeline says. "Let's
30 go to my house and eat lunch together. My servants cook enough food for ten people. There's always too much!"

"Thank you, Miss Adeline," Dorothy says. But Miles looks at the ground. He feels shy. Miss Adeline is very beautiful.

---

4 **to fill with tears** [fɪl wɪð 'tɪəz] sich mit Tränen füllen • 14 **immediately** [ɪ'miːdiətli] sofort • 15 **to report sb** [rɪ'pɔːt] jdn. melden • 15 **Head of Police** [ˌhed ɒv pə'liːs] Leiter der Polizei • 20 **handcuffs** *(pl)* ['hændkʌfs] Handschellen *(pl)* • 21 **Off you go then!** [ɒf juː 'gəʊ ðen] Gehen Sie schon!

Luckily, Dorothy has a lot to say. "Oh, Miss Adeline, we're so happy to see you. We were so worried that our uncle would find the locket. We had to hide it in the chicken coop and then our friend Nigel had to …"

Miss Adeline holds up her hand to stop Dorothy from 5 talking. But she isn't angry.

"Dear children," she says, "I don't even know your names."

Dorothy laughs. "Sorry," she says. "We're just so excited! It was very difficult to find you. I can't believe 10 we've succeeded!" Miss Adeline smiles and gives Dorothy a minute to calm down.

"I'm Dorothy Linton and this is my brother, Miles," Dorothy says.

"Very pleased to meet you," Miss Adeline says. "Now, if 15 you'd like to come home with me, you can wash and then tell me everything over lunch. How does that sound?"

"It sounds wonderful!" Dorothy says and takes Miles' hand.

"This is the best Easter ever," Miles whispers to her as 20 they follow Miss Adeline down the street and to her front door.

• • •

The children sit in Miss Adeline's dining room. They have washed and are now wearing fine clothes which Miss Adeline has borrowed from the neighbours' 25 children. Dorothy loves the pink dress she's wearing. She even has a matching ribbon in her hair.

The children feel very special as the butler serves them lunch. He was surprised to see them again, but now he is very polite. He even said sorry that he was rude to them. 30

1 **luckily** ['lʌkɪli] glücklicherweise • 11 **to succeed** [səkˈsiːd] Erfolg haben •
27 **ribbon** ['rɪbən] Band

"It's lovely to have you here," Miss Adeline says after Dorothy has told her how they found the locket and brought it to Belgrave Square. "I feel so sad when I eat lunch alone."

5 "Why do you eat alone?" Dorothy says. "Doesn't your family live in London?"

Miss Adeline looks very sad. "I'm an orphan," she says. "That's why the locket means so much to me. My father gave it to my mother."

10 "Is it his hair in the locket?" Miles asks. Now that he's eating the best meal of his life, he doesn't feel shy any more.

"Yes, it is," Miss Adeline says.

"When we noticed that there was a lock of hair inside
15 it, we knew it must be important to you," Dorothy says. "That's why we wanted to give the locket back to you, no matter what."

"Before that, we just wanted the reward money so we could run away," Miles says.

20 "Run away?" Miss Adeline asks.

"Yes," Dorothy says. She explains to Miss Adeline that they live with their cruel uncle instead of their grandma.

"How awful!" Miss Adeline says.

Miles tells her how sad they were when Uncle Bertram
25 sold their inheritance.

"We have lost everything that reminds us of our parents," he says sadly.

"That's not true," Miss Adeline says. "You have each other and your memories. You must always talk to each
30 other about your parents. That way you won't forget them."

"Do you have someone to talk to about your parents?" Miles asks.

1 **lovely** [ˈlʌvli] herrlich; wunderbar • 16 **no matter what** [nəʊ ˈmætər ˌwɒt] was auch immer passiert • 25 **inheritance** [ɪnˈherɪtəns] Erbe • 26 **to remind sb of sb** [rɪˈmaɪnd] jdn. an jdn. erinnern

Miss Adeline shakes her head. "I'm an only child."

Miles thinks for a minute. Then he says, "I have an idea! You can tell *us* about them!"

Miss Adeline's eyes fill with tears again. "You really are wonderful children," she says, "and you deserve a better 5 life." She looks thoughtful again. Then she is excited. "I know how to thank you for returning my locket. I'll organise train tickets for you both – First Class – and a servant to take you safely to your grandma's house. And I'll pay for both of you to go to school. Clever children 10 like you should be in school. And I'll send your grandma money every month until Miles is sixteen. That way, you'll have enough money for food and clothes!"

"Miss Adeline, you're so generous!" Dorothy says. "But your plan won't work. Uncle Bertram will never let us go 15 to Scotland. He says we must work for him forever, to pay him back."

"It's true," Miles says and he looks sadder than ever. Miss Adeline frowns.

Then she smiles. "I have made a decision," she says. 20 "You will both stay with me until it's time for you to go to Scotland. That means you will never have to see your awful uncle again."

"That's the most wonderful news I have ever heard!" Dorothy says. 25

"But Miss Adeline," Miles says, "what will we have to give you in return?" Living with Uncle Bertram has taught Miles that everything comes with a price.

But Miss Adeline smiles warmly. "I have only one request," she says. "You and your grandma must visit 30 me every Easter and Christmas, so that we can celebrate together."

"Sounds good to me!" Miles says.

---

14 **generous** [ˈdʒenərəs] großzügig • 19 **to frown** [fraʊn] die Stirn runzeln •
28 **to teach sb** [tiːtʃ] jdn. lehren • 30 **request** [rɪˈkwest] Bitte

Miss Adeline raises her glass. "I would like to propose a toast," she says. "To our new family: Dorothy, Miles, Grandma and me!"

Miles and Dorothy smile and raise their glasses too. 5 The butler enters the dining room and places bowls of ice cream on the table.

"Wow!" Miles says. "Ice cream on top of everything else!"

Everyone laughs. It's the best Easter Dorothy can 10 imagine, but she knows that next year will be even better.

1 **to raise one's glass** [ˌreɪz wʌnz ˈɡlɑːs] sein Glas erheben • 1 **to propose a toast** [prəˈpəʊz ə ˌtəʊst] einen Trinkspruch ausbringen • 7 **on top of everything else** [ɒn ˌtɒpˌəv ˈevriθɪŋ els] und dann auch noch; zu allem Überfluss

Exercises

1 Who is who? (Part 1)

Read part 1 and say who these sentences are about.

Dorothy | Miles | Uncle Bertram | Constable Owens |
Mrs Whitting | Robert | Mr Harris

1. This person is twelve years old.
2. This person is very tired and gives someone a piece of bread.
3. This person makes two children work for him and is often cruel to them.
4. These two persons are orphans and don't go to school.
5. When this person walks into the pawnshop, everyone stops talking.

2 Miles' money (Part 2)

Finish the sentences or choose the right answer.

1. Miles has got four half-pennies because …
   a) he stole them from Uncle Bertram's pawnshop.
   b) he sold ice cream in the park after church.
   c) he cleaned the neighbours' chicken coop.

2. What does Miles want to do with the half-pennies?
   a) He wants to buy train tickets to Scotland.
   b) He wants to save them to buy food the next day.
   c) He wants to buy ice cream after church.

3. When Uncle Bertram finds out about the money, he …
   a) hits Dorothy and Miles.
   b) sends them to work as mudlarks by the River Thames.
   c) says they have to stay at home and clean the house.

3 How do they feel? (Part 3)

a) *Put these sentences from part 3 in the right order. Number them from 1 to 7.*

☐ **A** "You have one hour to write a reply before I go out for dinner," Uncle Bertram says and leaves the kitchen.

☐ **B** Miles hides the locket in the neighbours' chicken coop, and the children enter the house through the back door. They look forward to warming up.

☐ **C** "You are stupid children!" Uncle Bertram shouts. "You and your brother will go to bed without eating dinner."

☐ **D** Dorothy and Miles are wet and cold and their backs hurt from working all day. But they're too excited to care.

☐ **E** "Miles and I want to live with Grandma," Dorothy says and her heart beats even faster.

☐ **F** Uncle Bertram ignores her question. "Give me what you found," he says and holds out his hand.

☐ **G** Uncle Bertram's face turns red. "What is this?" he says. "A plan to run away?"

b) *Choose at least three sentences from a) and draw an emoji for each to show how Miles, Dorothy or Uncle Bertram feel.*

4 Your turn: A letter to Grandma (Part 3)

Dorothy wants her grandma to know that she and Miles are planning to run away. She says to Miles:

"She needs to know that Uncle Bertram is cruel and won't let us go to Scotland. I won't say anything about the locket. We'll tell her about it when we get there."

Write Dorothy's letter to her grandma.

5 A word puzzle (Part 4)

a) *Find eight words from part 4 in the grid below.*

V	K	W	B	L	Y	H	M	J	Q	K	S
N	S	L	M	Y	O	S	A	Q	N	E	K
A	B	S	T	Z	K	L	R	V	N	O	D
W	Z	J	T	R	I	C	K	S	X	P	E
T	R	E	M	K	H	L	E	I	F	G	L
M	E	N	D	M	K	S	T	X	L	B	I
I	W	Z	I	M	U	J	F	O	A	D	V
P	A	W	N	S	H	O	P	X	U	L	E
Z	R	E	I	C	H	V	E	N	D	O	R
U	D	J	N	K	R	A	F	N	S	I	S
O	J	C	G	H	A	F	C	E	L	D	I

b) *Put the words from a) into the order of this text:*

Nigel works for a newspaper **(1)**. He **(2)** newspapers early in the mornings and in the evenings. When Nigel gives a newspaper to Mrs Simpkins, Dorothy gives him a **(3)**. As soon as Mrs Simpkins is gone, Dorothy gives Nigel some bread. Later, Dorothy and Miles talk to Uncle Bertram in the **(4)** room. Uncle Bertram **(5)** them: They don't have to work in the **(6)** that day. But they have to work as mudlarks. Uncle Bertram doesn't want the **(7)** for the locket, he wants to sell it on the black **(8)**.

6 What to do with the locket? (Part 5)

Match these sentence parts.

1. They can't tell the police that they have the locket

2. They have to work as mudlarks and can't go to the park

3. Tom and Frank are suspicious

4. Dorothy and Miles have to find the owner of the locket

5. They go to Nigel at the publisher's office

a) because Constable Owens is watching them.

b) because he can find out who the owner is.

c) because it won't be safe in the chicken coop for long.

d) because Constable Owens would ruin everything.

e) because Dorothy asks her friends many questions about the locket and the newspaper report.

7 Where? Who? What? (Part 6)

Choose a place and find the person/people who Dorothy and Miles (should) meet there. Then tell your partner what these people do to be nice or to be nasty to Dorothy and Miles. Take turns.

1. At church
2. At the pawnshop
3. In the graveyard
4. Near the butcher's shop
5. At the blacksmith's workshop

a) Nigel
b) Willie
c) Uncle Bertram
d) Frank and Tom
e) Mr Harris

8 Miss Adeline's house (Part 7)

a) *Are the sentences below right or wrong?*

	right	wrong
1. Dorothy and Miles hide, because Tom and Frank are across the street.		
2. When the children ring the bell, the butler lets them come into the house.		
3. A young man believes that the children want to help Miss Adeline.		
4. The butler pulls the children out of the house and tells them to go home.		
5. Constable Owens thinks that Dorothy has the locket.		

b) *Correct the sentences that are wrong.*

9 Lunch with Miss Adeline (Part 8)

Answer the questions in complete sentences.

1. How do Dorothy and Miles finally meet Miss Adeline?
2. What does Miss Adeline do for the children because they brought back her locket? Name at least two things.
3. What does Miss Adeline want the children and their grandma to do in the future?

10 Discussing the story (Post-reading)

a) *Do you like the story? Why? Why not? Talk about it in class.*

b) *Do you know any other stories that take place in the past?*

Solutions

Before you read the story

1 On the shores of the Thames

Lösungsvorschläge: plants; animals: dead fish, bird, dog; mud; treasures: coin, money, penny, jewellery (e. g. bracelet), clay pipe; rubbish: shoe, bag, bottle, broken bike, old food, old apple, hat, pen

2 The book cover

Lösungsvorschläge:

a) There are a girl and a boy in old and dirty clothes. The boy isn't wearing any shoes. He looks excited, but the girl looks worried.

b) They're on the shore of a river, probably under a bridge.

c) They're looking for treasures and have found something that is worth lots of money.

d) Maybe the story takes place in the past. The ships in the background look historical and the clothes look old. It's getting dark in the picture, so I think the scene takes place in the evening.

e) Maybe the story is about two poor children. Perhaps they find something that is worth lots of money, sell it and start a better life.

3 Finding a treasure

Lösungsvorschläge: I found some money in the street last year. I took it and bought some sweets with it. / I found a really nice book at school last week. There was a name in it, so I gave it back to that person.

Exercises

1 Who is who? (Part 1)

1. Dorothy,   2. Miles,   3. Uncle Bertram,   4. Dorothy and Miles,
5. Constable Owens

2 Miles' money (Part 2)

1. c,   2. c,   3. b

3 How do they feel? (Part 3)

a) 1. D,   2. B,   3. F,   4. A,   5. G,   6. E,   7. C

b) *Individuelle Schülerlösungen*